THE GUIDE BOOK

Where are guides? Who are guides? Why are guides?

By

River Lightbearer

With channeled contributions from Shiva and Pietkela, beings of light

This work is the sole intellectual property of Kimberly Ramsey-Winkler/River Lightbearer. It is available for personal use only. Digital versions cannot legally be loaned or given to others. The scanning or upload of this book for distribution is legally prohibited. No part of this book may be shared or reproduced without the express written permission of the author. To obtain permission, please contact the publisher at info@riverevolutions.com.

Nothing in this book is intended as medical, mental health, or legal treatment or advice. The author and publisher bear no responsibility or liability for the choices and decisions of the reader.

© 2021 Kimberly Ramsey-Winkler/River Lightbearer

Cover by Kim Ramsey-Winkler

Published by:
Vegan Wolf Productions
veganwolfproductions@gmail.com

Contents

1. River's Introduction — 1
2. A Few Introductory Words from Shiva — 7
3. Some Introductory Thoughts from Pietkela — 13
4. What Is a Guide? — 17
5. Forming the Connection — 35
6. Good, Bad, or Other: How to Know — 57
7. Honesty, Ethics, Consent, and Trust — 73
8. Afterword — 87
9. A Few Closing Words from Shiva — 89

Acknowledgements

Bibliography

About the Author

About RiverEvolutions

1 River's Introduction

For as long as I can remember—and probably longer than that—I have been surrounded by my guides. As a young child, I called them my "invisible friends," and responded very indignantly to anyone who made the mistake of calling them imaginary. These kind, gentle beings protected me and gave me the love and nurturing that was lacking in my life.

I opened to my guides through trauma. My childhood was, let's say, not a pleasant one. I was frequently rejected and punished for things I wasn't responsible for. Incidents of more serious trauma occurred at times, but even in my daily life, there was a sense that I wasn't safe, that the world—including my little corner of it in my home and neighborhood—was a dangerous place. I didn't feel that I had anyone to turn to. So, being a very young child who needed help and love, I reached out mentally for any support I could receive.

Our guides are always with us, from the moment of birth and sometimes from previous lifetimes. Fortunately, when my mind cried out, my own guides responded.

My first primary guide, a being of light, acted quickly to "cap my channel." That is, he put energetic protections in place so only the beings who were intended to work with me in this lifetime could connect and communicate with me. From that moment, my guides accompanied me everywhere. They spoke with me, played with me, allowed me to feel like someone loved me and cared if I was safe.

Even now, nearly five decades after they first showed themselves to me, they provide me with those feelings of love and safety. They speak with me, sometimes to encourage me to make the most ideal choices in my life, sometimes just to chat or joke around. Guides aren't always formal!

I can literally and legitimately say that if it weren't for my guides' constant presence and love in my life, I would not have survived this long.

Because of continuing trauma in my life, by the time I was around ten, my energetic vibration had fallen too low for my primary guide to work with me safely. In the interim, one of my spirit guides, Dominic, had taken over the role of primary guide until it was safe enough for my actual primary to work with me again. For the next quarter-century, I spoke with Dominic and my other guides, often wondering why I didn't outgrow them.

I didn't know anything about channeling until I was in my mid-thirties. At that time, I became friends with someone who practiced energy healing and channeling. He and his primary guide took me under their wings, figuratively speaking. Through the work I'd been doing to heal from my trauma, and the energy healing and other work my friend and his guide did with me, my vibration rose again to a safe level. My friend's guide facilitated my reconnection with my primary guide, who then introduced himself to me as Shiva.

My friend and his guide also taught me how to channel. Any time I say or type something one of my guides says, I am channeling. However, when most people think of channeling, they often mean the act of allowing a being to speak through you while your consciousness is "somewhere else." This is called trance channeling, and is something my friend and his guide, along with Shiva, taught me to do. I also do relayed channeling, which is the passing along of what Shiva or one of my other guides says to me.

All beings who act as guides have higher energetic vibrations than humans, but there are degrees of vibration. A guide will work with a human whose vibration is a match for theirs, meaning that someone whose vibration is lower might work with spirit guides, while someone whose vibration is higher might work with light beings or beings of light. (The chapter "What Is a Guide?" explains more about the different types of beings who might act as guides.)

Everyone has these beings around them. Most of us have more than one guide. For example, among my "crew," I have my primary guide along with a writing guide (who is helping me remember this list as I type), a body awareness guide, a spiritual growth guide, a Witchcraft guide, and a guide for my energy healing work. As new needs become apparent in our lives, additional guides might join us, sometimes permanently and sometimes just until we address that need.

That was the case for me during the writing of this book. I was informed that a being with whom I had been speaking for years was actually one of my guides, and that we would begin the transition to him becoming my primary guide and the one I channel. His name is Pietkela, and as I write this, we're in the transition process. He and Shiva both collaborated with me on this project.

Fortunately, guides don't go away unless there's no longer a reason for their presence. Shiva is still with me and I still work with him on certain things, including books such as this one (he isn't my writing guide; he's more of a collaborator). But Pietkela is now in the role of my primary guide. When I channel for others, sometimes I still channel Shiva, particularly if it's for someone who has had sessions with Shiva and me in the past, and sometimes I channel Pietkela.

However, not everyone knows their guides or how to work with them. And unfortunately, not all resources or practitioners that claim to teach people to connect with their guides do so in a safe and effective way.

This book is not intended as a how-to guide for connecting with and channeling your guides. I strongly recommend that you work with a legitimate, trained channel for either of those tasks, because then you have both a human and their guides keeping an eye out for any danger to you.

If you aren't able to access a trained channel to help you, I would recommend the books *Opening to Channel* by Sanaya Roman and Duane Packer, or, if you're able to find a copy, *Channeling: The Power of Connection* by Christopher S. Harris. (At last check, this book is out of print, and used copies are priced at outrageous sums.) I will also be publishing a book in the future, again in collaboration with Pietkela and Shiva, that will offer a safe and effective way to connect with your guides.

Meanwhile, the book you're reading now is meant to give you some insight into the world of working with guides, whether to channel for others or simply to receive guidance, love, and compassion in your own life. Some of what I address is based on questions I've answered on social media; some is based on what I feel is important to know if you are interested in or beginning to learn to work with your guides.

At the end of each chapter, I've included information I channeled directly from Shiva. When I first started outlining this book, I planned on using his input and Pietkela's as part of my research. It then occurred to me that in a book about guides and channeling, it made far more sense to include my guides' information in their own words. To indicate the information that was channeled in each chapter, I've put it in italics. In Shiva and Pietkela's introductions and closing statement, I've used regular font.

My intention is for this book to give you information and support as you consider or work to connect with your guides. It's based on my experiences, research, and on input from my guides, who gave me words when I was having trouble finding them, encouraged me, and gave me a figurative kick in the butt when I was resistant to working on this book because "I don't know enough."

Before we move on, a quick word about energetic vibration. I refer to vibration throughout this book, and mention both "high vibration" and "low vibration." High is not automatically good, and low is not automatically bad; they're simply different.

I've explained it in the past as being like an FM radio: 89.3 has a lower frequency than 107.9, but they're both perfectly decent radio stations. They're just different. (I'm just going to assume that even though streaming music is far more prevalent now than it was when I started using that analogy, my readers will still be at least somewhat familiar with FM radios!)

The difference between high and low vibration is a

matter of spiritual evolution, of conscious and unconscious choices made about how to navigate life, and of circumstances and environment. Your vibration can change throughout your life depending on thoughts, actions, and what's happening to and around you, as well as how you progress through your spiritual and life journeys.

Explaining the entire concept of energetic vibration is beyond the scope of this book, but since I do discuss it, I wanted to provide some information. My guides and I also want to assure you that the level of your vibration is not a judgment of who you are, how "good" you are, or anything of the kind. It's simply a quality, like the color of your hair, and like your hair color, it may change over time and can be changed intentionally.

I hope this book provides you with useful information about these beings we call "guides" and how they can help us in our lives.

2 A Few Introductory Words from Shiva

The connection between human and guide is a profound and beneficial thing. It can be a source of wisdom and knowledge, a source of joy and compassion, or all of the above.

Those of us beings who choose to act as guides have taken this step in order to facilitate our own spiritual growth and progress, and also to further yours. We wish to bring connection and community to the Universe as a whole, for the Universe is a Whole. No being exists in isolation. When one suffers, all, in some way, suffer; when one experiences joy, that joy resonates throughout the Universe.

We wish to add to the joy and love within the Universe.

Some of you have had negative or even frightening

experiences with beings who claimed to be your guides. They claimed falsely, for no benevolent being or true guide would engage in discourse or actions which cause pain or harm to another. It is an unfortunate truth that in the Universe, just as in your own world, there are those whose intentions are less than benign.

It is the hope of myself and other beings who work with humans that these experiences will not dissuade you from endeavoring to connect with your own true guides, nor from hearing or heeding the messages we bring. There are means of forming and strengthening these connections which will ensure your safety, and there are people and beings such as myself and my host, whom I know as Ganatram and you know as River Lightbearer, who wish to aid you in forming these connections in a manner safe for all involved.

This book does not delve into the details and, as you might say, "dos and don'ts" of connecting with your guides. That is for a later text which we shall produce soon. Rather, this book seeks to inform you of what types of beings you may encounter in your quest to connect and work with your guides, and cautions and considerations to bear in mind as you do so.

When you choose to work with your guides, all of us rejoice, for you are contributing to our work in the Universe. You are, in a sense, becoming one of us; for although you remain an incarnate human until your current life comes to an end, the messages we share with you and you share with others will in turn guide them to a higher path.

In your connection with your guides, you may choose to work with them only for your own growth and benefit. This is an acceptable choice, for as stated, each action and choice ripples throughout the Universe. Your own personal growth and learning add to the higher vibration throughout all planes. You may also choose to share your guide's messages with others through means such as verbal channeling or writing books. This, too, is an acceptable choice, provided that you choose based upon a desire to help others learn and grow rather than a desire to gain fame and accolades for your skills.

Even should you seek fame and accolades, your guides will not judge you, for that is not something we do. We accept the choices you make, though we may attempt to sway you toward more beneficial choices if something you decide might be a detriment to you or others. We do not abandon you if we disagree with your decisions. We do not become angry or threaten you if you do something against our wishes, for in your choices and your life path, your free will is paramount above all.

I am called Shiva, though that is only one name by which I am known and is a name I utilize with Ganatram because it is the name their mentor stated when suggesting that Ganatram seek my aid in a circumstance years ago. Previously, Ganatram had known me by other names, though those were not my true name any more than is Shiva. For me, and for those similar to me, names are a convenience we concede for the benefit of the humans with whom we work; they are not necessary for us.

I am a being of light, though this, too, is a designation taken for the benefit and understanding of humans, and is not the term by which I would otherwise identify myself. However, it is adequate, for in my true form I am light. I am energy. I have no physical form as you would understand it. I dwell in a plane of existence close to the Source of Creation, though I am not that being and do not claim to speak for it.

All of this is to say that I am different from you. However, I am not better. I am not superior. I merely have access to broader perspectives and wisdom than humans generally do. This is not a statement of superiority but of the reality of my existence. Humans also have perspectives and wisdom that I do not, and it is for this reason, in part, that I have chosen the path of guide.

Your guides and other beings who work with humans in other capacities do not do so because we are better or more enlightened, but because it is a mutually beneficial choice. Just as you learn and grow from working with us, so we learn and grow from working with you. Our understanding increases as does yours.

When you choose to work consciously with your guides, you embark upon a journey which will enrich your life and theirs, and likely the lives of other humans as well. The ground you gain and the insight and wisdom shared with and by you will enable you to shine a light for others who wish to grow and progress in their own journeys. This brings great benefit throughout the Universe.

In these pages, you will find information researched by Ganatram as well as channeled by them from me and from another of their guides, a being known as Pietkela. This information is intended to bring you an understanding of who guides are and why we have chosen this path, but it is not comprehensive and is not an ultimate statement of authority on the subject. Read with discernment and with attention toward your own intuition and inner knowing, for you know inside what is true for you. I encourage you to read with an open mind, but also to place what feels true and accurate to you ahead of what Ganatram and I have written.

May the information you find in these pages bring you benefit and learning, both about your guides and about your own path. In future, we shall bring you other publications which will teach and facilitate the connections between you and your guides and your ability to channel them. For now, know that your guides are with you, as they have been from the moment of your birth, and they wish to connect with you when you are ready to do so.

3 Introductory Thoughts from Pietkela

I shall speak concisely, for this book is primarily a collaboration between the human known as River Lightbearer and the being of light they know as Shiva. However, I have contributed and have therefore been asked to add my thoughts.

In the Universe, there are far more beings than only humans. Many of you know this already, and yet find it odd that we might wish to communicate with and aid you. Those who do not find it odd may still doubt or question that one of these beings would communicate with them specifically.

You are part of a Whole. The Universe is not a collection of isolated beings but a community of sentience and knowing. Some of you are willing and eager to become part of this community. Working with your guides is one method of doing so.

I am known as Pietkela, though this is not my true

name but rather an approximation of it translated into a form which may be spoken by humans. In other quarters, I am known in other ways.

Although River, in their introduction to this book, refers to me as a being of light, that is not a designation I use for myself. I have allowed them to use it here for the sake of convenience; however, in my direct work with them, I have refused to identify the type of being they might consider me. As I have explained to them, at times their need to name and categorize people and things is an obstacle to their growth, so I have chosen to place them in a position where some of the categorization they desire is unavailable to them.

I do not do this to cause them pain or to be "mean." Rather, it is my role as their guide to aid in their spiritual progression and healing journey. Their reliance on names and labels interferes with this progress at times. I give an opportunity for them to break free of that structure. It is an opportunity they have chosen to accept; had they not, I would not have persisted in refusing to identify what "type" of being I am.

In each of your lives, guides are present, albeit often without your knowledge. In each of your lives, these beings offer opportunities to further your growth, your healing, and your understanding. Whether you accept these opportunities is entirely your decision, for we do not force anything upon you. We do not wish to subjugate nor to command, but to work with you in a way that benefits you, us, and the Universe as a Whole.

Some of you have experience in speaking and working with your guides. Some of you have had negative experiences with entities masquerading as guides, for just as there are humans who have no one's best interests in mind, so are there entities throughout the Universe who seek to cause difficulties or to deceive others. In part of this book, you will learn to distinguish those entities from those of us who are true guides.

River and I also work together to enable people to connect with their guides without fear of interference by these entities, and it is recommended that if you wish to connect consciously to your guides, you avail yourself of assistance from a channel and being who will guard against such interference. This assistance, of course, need not come from us. There are many others who provide similar service.

The Universe is changing. Your world is changing. The connections between you and your guides, and between you and other beings who communicate with humans while not acting as guides, will aid in ensuring that these changes bring benefit and growth. We have created this book and are creating other resources to facilitate these connections so that we may work together.

Read these words with discernment. Indeed, in any resource or teaching, in any service from another, use discernment, for you know within yourself whether something is true and beneficial for you. We do not seek to state that we know better than you, nor that you must do anything particular. Listen to your Core Self, for that is where your knowledge and wisdom reside. Should that Self tell you that the words within these pages are true, we are pleased to have been of service.

4 What Is a Guide?

The Role of a Guide

In the Universe, we are far from the only sentient beings who exist. Humans actually are a very small percentage of all the consciousnesses in the Universe, and we're only aware of the existence of a few of the other types of beings.

Many of those beings, however, are aware of us. Some of them are curious about humans, or intrigued by us, or simply want to observe and see what we do. They don't choose to work with humans, and some aren't even particularly interested in us. Others, however, do want to interact with us and even work with us closely.

There are beings or entities who want to bring us harm, or at least not bring us any benefit, for one reason or another. I generally use "beings" to refer to those with benevolent intent, and "entities" to refer to those with neutral or malevolent intentions, and that is how I will use those terms throughout this book. Sometimes they simply don't operate with the same system of values and understanding as us, so to us their behavior may appear malevolent, but to them, it's completely acceptable.

There are also beings who want to benefit us. To help us grow and evolve as a species and as individuals. These beings are on their own path of spiritual growth and development, and working with humans is part of that path. Some beings interact with multiple humans, simply providing messages and information through whatever means are available. Others choose to work closely with one or a very few individual humans. The latter are referred to as guides.

As we humans go through our lives, sometimes we get stuck. We need guidance or information. We could benefit from advice and suggestions. We also live lives in which sometimes we face dangerous situations, whether or not we're aware of the danger at the time. Something as simple as taking a walk or driving a car can lead to negative results.

Wouldn't it be amazing to have someone with us all the time who could give us guidance and advice? Someone to keep an eye on us and steer us away from threats, and support us through the aftermath of situations we aren't able to avoid?

Those are the roles of a guide. Guides are beings who have chosen to continue their own spiritual growth and progression by working directly with individual humans. A guide both teaches a human and learns from them, because working with a guide isn't a one-way street. Even though guides are more spiritually developed and have higher energetic vibrations than humans, they aren't better than us. They have as much to gain from working with us as we have from working with them.

A guide exists in a different existential plane than humans. They have higher energetic vibration and are not incarnate; that is, they don't have bodies, even though they can choose to appear as if they do. Instead, they exist in a form of pure energy, which some humans may consider light. These beings have learned to cross into our plane of existence, or at least to transmit their messages to our plane, in order to work with us.

Before incarnation, at a soul level, we humans plan to learn specific lessons during our lifetime. This doesn't mean we're choosing to go through hell to learn them, though, despite what some spiritual practitioners claim! Rather, it means that our souls know what we need to learn and what growth we need to accomplish in order to continue our spiritual progression through this life and lifetimes to come. It's important to note, though, that once we incarnate we have free will. We might choose not to learn those lessons after all.

Even though we may not be consciously aware of our guides, and very likely aren't consciously aware of what those soul-chosen lessons are, our guides know. They'll present us with non-harmful opportunities to learn those lessons if we choose on some level, conscious or not, to go forward with them. A guide will never put you at risk or in a situation that might harm you so you can learn. Rather, they'll give you nudges toward beneficial ways to gain the knowledge and understanding you need.

Often, a guide is connected to a specific individual human for that human's entire lifetime, though some guides may work with more than one human during a given time span. (At least as humans measure time. Time operates differently from guides' perspectives.) The guide and human may be connected through more than one human lifetime. The connection remains even as the soul

passes out of one body and into another. The longer a guide and human work together, the more fluid and comfortable the work becomes, particularly when the human channels.

Different guides have different interests, understanding, purpose, and areas of expertise. Like humans, guides are individuals with their own views and personalities. A guide is likely to work with a human with whom they share those things or whose interests and purpose are complementary to the guide's. Sometimes this is a "chicken and egg" thing; if a guide and human have worked together for multiple lifetimes, the human's interests and purpose may be formed, at least on a subconscious level, through the input of their guides.

Even if a human's needs and purpose aren't part of the guide's purview, the guide will find ways to help the human gain the knowledge and understanding they need. If you've ever felt a nudge to go into a certain store and found exactly the right book about a subject you've felt drawn to study, for example, that nudge very likely came from one or more of your guides.

I recently experienced one of the strongest nudges and strings of "coincidence" I've ever had. My path with channeling and my guides took a turn during a trip to Florida in early 2021, while I was still researching this book. On that trip, I "accidentally" found my way to a metaphysical shop in Cocoa Village.

I was walking back to my car after a stroll down one of the streets in the village, and I was pretty eager to get in the car and get home after a fairly long afternoon. But something in the window of a shop caught my eye. I decided to go into the shop to take a closer look.

The shop was part of a tiny mall, which contained four or five stores total. I glanced into the door of the shop that had caught my attention and decided I didn't want to go in after all, so I started to go back to the street. But something inside me said no, I needed to go to the end of the corridor to see what else was there. (To be honest, I was hoping to find a restroom.)

At the end of the corridor, there was the metaphysical shop. I almost didn't go in, because the name of the shop included a word that sometimes irritates me, for no real reason other than that people tend to overuse it. Again, I started to go back to the street, but something told me to go in, so in I went. In that shop, I had a conversation with the owner, who was the one to tell me that I would be working with a guide other than Shiva.

Overall, it was a very positive interaction, and I felt the truth behind what she'd said. But on the way back to the house where I was staying, I asked Shiva, "Is it true? It feels like it is, but it also sounded kind of ego-strokey, so I want to make sure."

Shiva confirmed it. That was when I learned that Pietkela, a being with whom I'd spoken off and on for about the same length of time I'd been channeling Shiva, was actually one of my guides and was the being to whom the woman in the shop had been referring.

Who Are Guides? Why Are Guides?

All humans have guides, and it is very rare for a human to have only one. While most, if not all, humans have a primary guide who is able to assist the human with generally living their life and pursuing their purpose, a person will also have guides for specific tasks. As I said in the introduction to this book, I have a guide who specifically helps me write, one who helps me with body awareness (if he tells me to sit up straight one more time, I might scream...), one who helps with the energy healing work I do, and one who works with me in my chosen spiritual path of Witchcraft. A friend of mine has a guide who specifically helps them with digital graphic design.

Whether a guide is a primary or one who assists with a specific type of task, they choose to work with a human whose life purpose is aligned with theirs.

There are several types of beings who might act as guides, though not all beings of each type choose that path. Some guides have previously incarnated, either because it's part of their existential path or by choice, and have lived in our world. Others are from other dimensions and have never incarnated. Some may be angels or masters, though those beings are more likely to deliver messages to various humans rather than acting as guides for individual humans. Some don't fit any of these categories.

The beings who most commonly act as guides are spirit guides, light beings, and beings of light. Most people have and work with spirit guides, as they're the beings with the vibration most compatible with the vibration of most humans. They also, due to having been incarnate as humans themselves, are the ones easiest for humans to relate to. Some humans work with light beings; fewer work with beings of light, though that number is increasing as more people turn to spiritual growth and energy work which raises their vibration.

Various books and resources may define each type of being differently, and some don't recognize the existence of all of these types. I use the descriptions and definitions I learned from the mentor who taught me to channel, which are also listed in his book, *Channeling: The Power of Connection.*

Spirit Guides

The spirit guide is probably the type of being most familiar to humans. A spirit guide is a soul who has usually lived multiple lifetimes as an incarnate human, and has either reached the end of their incarnation cycle, meaning they are able to progress in their spiritual growth without needing to incarnate again, or has chosen to suspend that cycle to assist other humans. A spirit guide may choose to work with a human with whom they had a connection in the human's current lifetime or a previous lifetime.

Spirit guides aren't ghosts! A ghost is the energetic remnant of a human who has died and whose soul hasn't yet crossed over into what my guide Shiva refers to as "the Between." Ghosts are often stuck to the location in which they died, or another location that had a strong meaning for the person. A ghost might speak to and even give advice to humans, but they aren't guides, have low energetic vibrations, and may cause harm.

In fact, being around a ghost for a period of time can drain the energy from a living person. This isn't usually intentional on the ghost's part; it's simply the result of their vibration being as low as it is. Just as a living person with a low energetic vibration might cause you to feel drained or exhausted just by their presence, so does a ghost.

A spirit guide, on the other hand, usually has crossed to the Between after their death in their last incarnation. They have worked on their own spiritual growth and have chosen to work with another human so that both might grow and learn. Spirit guides have the lowest vibration of the beings who act as guides, but their vibration is still higher than that of most, if not all, incarnate humans.

When your spirit guide is present, you'll feel uplifted and energized rather than exhausted and drained.

Because spirit guides have lived human lifetimes, they may act like they did in life or as if they're still human. Essentially, they are. This means they may speak casually, use slang, and even joke around with you, though never in a cruel way. A spirit guide, like any other guide, will never intentionally say something hurtful or give you suggestions that might cause harm.

I work with four spirit guides. One of them, Dominic, shared a previous incarnate lifetime with me, and chose to continue working with me and being my friend after he suspended his incarnation cycle. He has a dry sense of humor and can be a bit sarcastic at times, but he is still a guide, and only jokes with or playfully teases me because he knows I enjoy it. Even though he offers me guidance and support, I think of him more as a close friend or even a brother than a higher-level being, and he's okay with that.

Light Beings

Another type of being that might work with humans is a light being. Just as humans are a species, so to speak, so are light beings; while each of them is different in personality, knowledge, and interests, there are commonalities among them as well.

When someone speaks of communicating with a collective of beings, often the beings in the collective may be light beings. Collectives, however, don't act as guides, but rather convey messages to benefit humanity as a whole. It is also possible that individual members of a collective may act as guides separate from or in conjunction with their work with the collective, but the collective as a whole won't be a guide to an individual human.

In general, light beings don't live incarnate lifetimes unless they choose to do so to further their spiritual growth or simply to "see what it's like." Because light beings have not lived as humans, they may seem odd or alien to us. They don't think or behave like us for the most part. But as with incarnation, the way they act is a choice, and some will choose to act more human for the comfort of the human with whom they're working.

Light beings have a higher energetic vibration than spirit guides, and dwell closer to the Ultimate Source of Creation than spirit guides do. Keep in mind, though, that "dwell" and "close are figurative terms. Since all of these beings are comprised of pure energy, they don't literally live anywhere. However, it is true that the higher the vibration, the closer the being—whether human or not—is to Source.

Two of my guides are light beings, and their roles—and to some extent their personalities—are very similar. One identifies himself as my guide for inner spiritual growth, while the other is my guide for external spiritual learning. Because they know it reassures me, and because they took some cues from characters I had created for a teen urban fantasy series I was working on, they speak and behave in a more humanistic manner than some light beings would.

Beings of Light

The third type of being that most commonly acts as a guide is a being of light. The term "being of light" is more of a category than an identification. Unlike humans or light beings, who are individuals but part of overall species, each being of light may be said to be a species unto themself. However, all beings of light share the commonality of existing in a state of pure energy that humans may perceive as light, and beings of light work with light and energy, so humans use the term to designate the work and existential state rather than the beings themselves.

To put it more simply, saying a being is a "being of light" is like saying a human is a "being of flesh and bone." It's a description, not the term for the species itself.

Beings of light have the highest energetic vibration of the beings who are most likely to act as guides and are the closest to the ultimate Source. They have access to a vast range of wisdom, knowledge, and perspectives, and have chosen to share these things with humans as part of their own spiritual growth as well as to aid humans in ours. They exist in a different plane or dimension from humans, but are easily able to cross into our realm to work with us.

Beings of light rarely incarnate, though like light beings, they may choose to do so in order to experience incarnation and better understand humans. Even if they've had this experience, though, beings of light often come across as particularly alien or odd to humans because of the intense differences in how they perceive the Universe and in their experiences of existence.

While a being of light, like other guides, may choose to act and speak in a certain way for the comfort of the human with whom they're working, they're less likely to do so. A human who is connected with a being of light is likely to have reached a point in their own spiritual evolution at which they can accept the differences and discomfort more easily, so the being of light will often choose to maintain these differences to push the human's comfort zone. This isn't done with the intention of making the human uncomfortable, but rather to help them continue to grow and to not stay stagnant within the limits of their comfort.

My guide Shiva is a being of light. He tells me he is formed of energy that has no form, and that to human perception that energy appears as light. I've known him since I was a child, though I didn't learn until adulthood that he was my guide. (I didn't learn until adulthood that any of the beings I'd been communicating with all of my life were my guides.) Even at times when my energetic vibration was too low for him to safely be in direct contact with me, he's been there, watching over and protecting me.

He is the guide I first learned to channel, and sometimes the intensity of his vibration, along with his phrasing and the changes in my voice and mannerisms when I allow him to speak directly through me causes people discomfort or even fear. But he is benevolent. Even people who have felt uncomfortable have told me when Shiva's present, they feel a sense of overwhelming *goodness*. That's the sense I've had from him since he first evidenced himself to me when I was a young child, three or four years old.

Over our time of working together, although he doesn't perceive things the way a human does or behave even remotely like a human, he has learned to joke around with me and even exhibit a sense of humor and sarcasm, partly because he enjoys learning how humans behave and partly because he knows I feel loved and comfortable when he acts that way.

Not All Beings Are Guides

Other beings exist who communicate with humans at times but rarely act as guides. They are also furthering their own spiritual growth, as well as helping humans further ours, by conveying messages and offering guidance, but because they speak to a wide range of humans and don't work closely with any, they wouldn't be considered guides.

The types of being with which most people are familiar are angels and archangels. Angels and archangels, like the beings I've already mentioned, exist as energy on a different plane from humans and have a higher energetic vibration; they're also closer to the Ultimate Source, on a similar level to light beings or beings of light.

Contrary to what some believe, an angel is not a deceased human; angels are a different type of consciousness altogether. Angels may take on a human form to communicate with us more easily, but they don't fully incarnate and often they relay messages through means other than taking on a physical-looking form. Although humans often mention having a "guardian angel," a being who acts as what we might consider to be a guardian angel is more likely to be a guide, sometimes a spirit guide who previously incarnated as a family member to the human.

Ascended humans, also referred to as ascended masters, also communicate with humans at times, though more rarely than angels. An ascended human is one who, through their incarnation cycle, has reached an evolutionary level at which they were able to transcend incarnating and exist as pure energy. After this point, they may choose to incarnate, but it's entirely a choice. While an ascended human may communicate and interact with humans, they almost never act as guides, because it simply is not part of their spiritual journey.

People whose spiritual path includes working with the elements of Air, Fire, Water, and Earth may be familiar with Elementals. These beings are associated with one of the four elements (five if one includes Spirit). While an Elemental may assist someone in working with the element with which they're connected, and may even form a connection with the human, Elementals rarely act as guides. They have the ability to choose to do so, however. Elementals do not incarnate.

Beings don't always operate as individuals. As discussed in the section on light beings, some beings form collectives or societal groups. A collective may consist of anywhere from a dozen beings to thousands, working in conjunction with one another, which allows them access to broader knowledge and perspectives than they might have individually. It also allows them to communicate with multiple humans simultaneously.

The beings within a collective have generally chosen to work in this way as part of their spiritual growth, so are unlikely to incarnate since there is no need for them to do so. A collective as a whole will also not act as guides to individual humans. An individual being from within a collective may choose to become a guide to an individual human while also remaining part of the collective.

This is uncommon, but is the case with my guide Pietkela, who is part of a collective he calls The Collaboration. Because I am an impermeable channel, meaning only my own guides are able to speak with and work with me, Pietkela is the only member of this collective with whom I speak. Some of his work with me is individual, but some, particularly some of what I channel from him, is on behalf of The Collaboration.

A human who channels may be able to channel information and messages from any of the above types or groups of beings, regardless of whether a being is that human's guides. This depends in part on whether the human's connection to their own guides is permeable or impermeable. A human with an impermeable connection is unlikely to be able to channel from collectives or other beings who are not their guides. I'll talk more about permeable and impermeable connections in the next chapter.

Humans are also sometimes able to channel their higher selves. This allows them access to a broader range of wisdom than their day-to-day self might have, and isn't dependent on what type of connection the human has with their guides. However, someone's higher self cannot be their guide because it is an aspect of the person, albeit a wiser and more evolved aspect.

To Sum Up...

Just as not all beings act as guides, not all guides connect and interact with a human in the same way. Some guides work with us on a daily or regular basis. They might be just as likely to advise us on the best clothing for the weather or the best route to take to work as on our spiritual growth or healing journey. These are the guides who are most likely to have been with us all our lives, even if we haven't been aware of it.

Other guides show up as a human progresses in their spiritual growth and raise their vibration through spiritual and healing work. These guides often come specifically to help us with further growth and healing, and that's usually what they advise us about, though some may also become daily contributors to our lives.

Although a guide's guidance might seem to be your own intuition, in general when your intuition "speaks" to you, you feel it within your own body. Guidance and information from a guide, however, feels external, whether you're hearing them speak to you or simply receiving a "nudge."

No matter whether they're a daily presence or only speak to you occasionally, your guides are always with you. Even if you aren't aware, they're there, and you only need to speak to them to receive a response. These beings want to help and support you in your growth, learning, and healing; all you need to do is ask. And asking is necessary, because they will never violate your free will by giving you support or information without your request.

How Do You Know Your Guides Are There?

- You feel someone watching over, supporting, and protecting you
- At times, you've felt a strong urge to go someplace you haven't been before—and there, you've found answers to your questions or needs.
- Sometimes answers and solutions come to you "out of nowhere"
- When you're struggling, you feel or "hear" reassurance and don't know where it comes from
- At times, you hear a "little voice" in your mind advising you about your course of action. Maybe you believed it was your own voice.
- Your dreams include conversations with people that answer questions or resolve concerns you've been having
- You feel like someone or something is guiding you to what's most beneficial for you
- You had "imaginary" friends who knew more than you did as a child, and you didn't outgrow them
- You believe you have guides

A Few Words from Shiva

Guides choose to work with humans for the benefit of both the human and the being. It is part of a path to spiritual growth for both.

There are several different types of beings who work with humans. Among them are spirit guides; beings of light; angels; light beings, and ascended masters. Not all of these beings act as guides to individual humans, however. Some simply speak with humans, but are not their guides.

A guide is a being who has chosen to work specifically with one or more individual humans. This is more of a collaboration than instruction. The guides both teach and learn from the human. When this occurs, it is often something determined at the human's soul level prior to incarnation, and the human and being may have worked together in previous of the human's lifetimes.

The purpose of a guide is to facilitate and contribute to the spiritual growth and understanding of the human. For this reason, a guide may advise a human to make choices or take courses of action the human would not have considered on their own, and which may cause mild discomfort for the human. This, too, is not done out of malice, but without pushing and discomfort, growth does not occur. A guide will not push the human beyond the human's capabilities, though the human may feel incapable, and will not advise any actions which would be harmful to the human. They may, however, push beyond the human's comfort and advise actions which feel frightening to the human.

However, a guide will also support the human in following that course or making that decision. Guides do not tell you what to do and then leave you to do it. We remain with you to offer support, assistance, and further guidance as requested. You are never alone in following guidance given to you by the beings with whom you work.

We are always with you to support you in following what we have advised, or following whatever course of action you choose even should it run counter to what we have suggested, for beings do not judge you. We do not condemn you for ignoring or refusing our guidance. We will support you in any course that does not involve intentional harm to yourself or others.

Truly, even if you choose a course which involves intentional harm, we will not judge you for it, though we will strongly advise you against it and may make effort to prevent you from following that course. However, that advice or action comes without judgment and merely from our wish to protect you and others and to bring you benefit and positive growth.

5 Forming the Connection

Your Guides Are Always There

Whether or not you've formed a conscious, intentional connection with your guides, they're with you from the moment you're born. These beings may have been with you in previous lifetimes or you may have connected with them on a soul level between incarnations, so they're ready to work with you in this lifetime. No particular actions on your part are needed for them to be there.

If you haven't intentionally formed a connection, you aren't able to consciously work with your guides and may not even be aware they exist. The benefits these beings bring through speaking with you and offering you guidance in other ways isn't available on the same level. They'll still guide you, because that's their role in your life, but it will more likely take the form of the "little voice in your mind" that encourages or discourages certain actions, or "coincidences" that lead you to the people and resources you need.

The process of connection between a guide and a human takes work on both sides. In order to work with a human, a guide must alter their perceptions and their vibrational frequency. This takes conscious effort, and is one reason not all beings choose to act as guides.

On the human's side, awareness of the intention for connecting with the guide is necessary. Guides don't exist to tell you what to do, to do everything for you, or to absolve you of responsibility for your life; if that's what you hope to gain, you may not be ready yet for a conscious connection. It's important to avoid becoming overly reliant on your guides, because they aren't with you to control your life or make everything easier on you. They're with you to help you live your own life and make your own decisions, even the tough ones.

Opening by Chance

Connecting with your guides and opening to channel may happen by chance or by choice and may be complete or incomplete. Opening by chance often occurs when the human has experienced trauma, particularly if they're a child. An adult who experiences trauma or abuse may also connect with their guides by chance, but connection being sparked by trauma more commonly occurs for children.

When a child is being harmed or neglected, in their need, they might "cry out" mentally for help. Their guides will attempt to answer this call both to support and help the child and to protect them against connection with malevolent entities. If they choose to make the child aware of their presence and communicate with the child, the guides may initially represent themselves as imaginary friends because it's easier for the child to understand and is less likely to frighten them. The child's highest-vibration guide may put energetic protections in place to ensure that only the beings who are truly the child's guide are able to connect and communicate with them; this is called impermeability.

Opening by chance doesn't always occur due to emotional trauma. A physical trauma, particularly an accident or illness that results in injury to the brain, can also cause the human to open to their guides.

This is more of a risk for the human. The injuries and the energy being diverted to healing can leave them less able to discern whether they're connecting with their genuine guides or with negative entities. It can also leave them more open to communication from beings and entities that are not their guides. As with someone who has experienced trauma, the guides of a human who has opened due to injury or illness will try to put protections in place, but this may be more difficult.

Another, less benign, way in which opening by chance might occur is through poorly done or incorrect spiritual practices, or practices performed without having adequate protections in place.

There are a number of spiritual and religious paths that involve communicating with other beings or have components such as meditation, prayer, or spells, that might lead to these connections. Spiritual practices that are done without full knowledge or understanding of their purpose and safe methods, or with a less benevolent intention, can open humans to contact from malevolent entities. This is particularly true if it's done by or for someone who is seeking power to hold over others, or by someone who simply is ignorant of the proper methods and reasons for doing it.

Even when the practice is done with benign intentions by someone who is aware of the correct methods and reasons, if protections aren't in place for the people involved and the space in which it takes place, malevolent entities may still come through. These entities often represent themselves as benign or benevolent, and fooling humans can be easy for them. Chapter 6 has more information about how to tell whether you're connecting with your own guides or with an entity.

When someone connects with their guides due to trauma, illness, or injury, obviously they have little to no choice in how it happens. The guides are there to support them however they need, and in these cases the guides determine the nature and process of the connection. It is still possible for someone opening under these circumstances to end up connected with an entity rather than their guides, though it's less likely because the guides act to protect the person by connecting with them and are therefore more likely to take precautions.

If someone opens by chance through a spiritual practice, they likewise may have little to no choice in it. Their intention in engaging in the practice is probably not connecting with their guides or other beings. They might be seeking to gain some type of power, or to hand their power over to a deity. Maybe they're trying to cause changes in their life, or maybe they just want to try the "new shiny" they've heard so much about.

In these cases, particularly if gaining or giving power is a focus, the person may not even reach their own guides. The call they unknowingly put out through these practices is just as likely to be answered by entities who have their own desire for power or who just like to cause trouble for humans. The human's genuine guides may not be able to make a connection in time to protect the human from interference by these entities. Opening by chance under these circumstances is much more dangerous than a chance connection due to trauma, illness, or injury.

Opening by Choice

While some people connect with their guides and open to channel by chance, others do so by choice. They may have heard about their guides from practitioners or through their own spiritual studies, or maybe they've simply felt a "nudge" that leads them to choosing to make the connection intentionally and actively. Connecting by choice can be less risky, but it still necessitates precautions and protections.

When someone chooses to connect, it's vital that the process be done in the safest manner possible. This means having guidance or instruction from an experienced, trained channel who is working with a genuine guide with a high enough energetic vibration to protect against unwanted or negative entities during the process.

The guidance might be in the form of a book, an online or in-person class, or a private session, and often includes a guided meditation led by the trained channel. Optimally, it will happen in person or over a real-time video connection during which the channel and their guide can see and interact with you and you can report what you're experiencing. But if this isn't possible, a book, recorded meditation, or video instruction can be equally safe and effective, provided it was produced by someone trained in channeling and in helping others connect with their guides.

It's also important to set aside your ego. If you're trying to connect with your guides due to a belief that you'll be more powerful or you'll gain accolades and attention, even if this belief isn't conscious, you risk attracting entities who are drawn to those thoughts and the energetic patterns that accompany them. The primary reason for choosing to connect with your guides needs to be your own spiritual growth and learning, not what others might think and say about you or any power and attention you might gain.

Who Do You Meet?

Usually when someone opens by choice under optimal conditions, they encounter their highest-vibration guide first. This isn't always the case, however. Sometimes the human's energetic vibration isn't high enough yet to tolerate the vibration of their highest guide, so another of their guides will step in to act as an intermediary.

An intermediary will act as the human's primary guide temporarily, providing guidance and opportunities for spiritual growth and other inner work that will help the human raise their vibration. The intermediary might also make tweaks to the human's energy system to facilitate raising their vibration. When the human is ready to work with their highest guide, the intermediary will step aside, though they're likely to still be present to work with and speak with the human. There's no set timeframe for this process; it depends on the human's vibrational frequency in the beginning and on how willing and able they are to do the work to raise their vibration.

Although when I first connected with my guides, my guide of highest vibration, Shiva, was the first to connect with me, over time the abuse and other trauma I experienced lowered my vibration to a point at which it was no longer safe for him to work with me directly. At that time, one of my spirit guides, Dominic, stepped into the role of primary guide as an intermediary. He helped me through the trauma, both with his own wisdom and guidance and by conveying support and guidance from Shiva, for almost thirty years.

Finally, through a series of "coincidences," I met my mentor. He and his guide, as I put it jokingly at the time, "conspired" with Shiva to bring my vibration back to a safe level through energy healing, yoga practice, and sessions in which my mentor channeled his guide for me. When I was deemed ready, my mentor's guide made the necessary adjustments in my energy system so that I could begin working with Shiva again. At that time, Dominic returned to his original role as my writing and Witchcraft guide.

Whether you connect with your highest-vibration guide first or an intermediary, this being will modify your energy system to enable you to connect and work with all of your guides, even ones you aren't quite ready to meet yet. These modifications might take the form of restoring your energy system through techniques similar to what a human might use in energy healing, or creating additional energetic "threads" or channels through which the human and their guides will connect.

These changes are generally subtle, and often the human isn't aware of them, though they won't be made unless the human gives their agreement. As with anything involving guides, connection requires free will.

When someone opens by chance, they also might encounter their highest-vibration guide first, but not necessarily. Trauma, illness, and injury can cause someone's energetic vibration to drop, resulting in them having too low a vibration to be able to tolerate their highest-vibration guide at first. This is another case in which another guide might take the role of intermediary until the human's vibration rises enough to work safely with their highest-vibration guide.

Knowingly and intentionally connecting with your guides requires trust, readiness, and openness. You choose to undergo the process of connection and opening, but if you try too hard to control how the process goes, you'll end up partially or completely blocking the connection. Even if you've already connected with your guides by chance, you can go through an intentional process, again being sure to have guidance and instruction from a trained channel, to solidify the connection and begin consciously working with your guides.

Once you've connected with your guides, you'll be able to communicate with them whenever you choose. You don't have to be in trance to speak with or work with them, though a trance state, usually the alpha brainwave state, makes the communication easier and is necessary when channeling.

My guides show up for conversations with me when I'm writing, or watching TV, or driving my car. For me, since I grew up considering them friends, having a conversation with them is very similar to having a conversation with my human friends, except that I "hear" them in my mind rather than with my ears.

Perceptions, Impressions, and Labels

When you connect with your guides, you may have certain perceptions of them. Humans love to label and categorize, and to some extent, our guides support that because they know it helps us feel comfortable. For example, a guide's true physical appearance may be, as one person's guide described themself, "akin to a spiral galaxy," or pure energy, or they may not even have a physical appearance. But if the human feels more comfortable being able to visualize or see a physical form, the guide may give themself a humanistic appearance or another form that the human will find comforting. This isn't their actual form, but just a perception they give the human to put the human more at ease.

Similarly, the name and gender a guide gives, or which a human perceives for a guide, is often chosen by the guide to help the human feel more comfortable. In the higher planes of existence where these beings dwell, gender doesn't exist, and since these beings may exist as pure energy and have no physical form, biological sex doesn't exist either.

Names are a bit trickier. All beings have names, but those names may not be comprehensible or translatable in human language. It's rare for a being to give their true name when working with a human; they literally might not be able to do so because of the difference in language forms, or they may choose not to because the name is complex or would sound or feel uncomfortable for the human.

Since we humans like to be able to identify things and have something to call those with interact with, beings will usually choose a gender and name. A spirit guide might choose based on one of their incarnate lifetimes or from what they detect will be most comfortable for the human. A light being or being of light is more likely to determine their name and gender from what they're able to pick up from the human's thoughts and past experiences or on what they deem will help the human feel most comfortable.

On the other hand, if a human's spiritual growth and life path necessitates them letting go of their preconceptions of labels, names, and gender, a guide might refuse to give a name or present themself in any particular way other than their true form. They may even opt not to let the human perceive their true form, but only to hear their words and know they're a benevolent being. How the human feels is important, but a guide's role is to help the human push comfort zones in order to progress in their life path.

Even if a guide gives you a name, gender, appearance, etc. when you first connect with them, this might not be how you perceive and identify them the entire time you work together. Since these identifiers are chosen based on the human's needs, comfort, and understanding, and all of those things can change over time, the guide may choose to change their name and other identifying factors as the human changes.

This can be particularly true if the human is a child when the first connection occurs. When my guides came to me, I was only two years old. I couldn't conceptualize any beings other than humans, and in fact barely had a concept of other humans. Names were definitely not something I completely understood. So two of my guides took the names of characters in a Saturday morning TV show I watched, and Shiva allowed me to think of him as "Jesus," since I was raised in a nominally Christian household and at least had a sense that Jesus was a hugely good presence—which was also how I perceived this guide.

As I got older and gained more understanding of people, names, and life in general, the names by which I knew my guides changed. Sometimes I chose their names; other times, they gave me names to call them. The name Shiva was told to me by the mentor who taught me how to channel, because that was the name by which he knew this being.

My guides themselves didn't change. Only the way they allowed and enabled me to perceive them changed based on my needs and comprehension.

The Connection Evolves

While my individual guides remained the same beings regardless of whether they changed the names by which I knew them, the "cast of characters," so to speak, changed from time to time. Many of the "invisible friends" I had as a young child left after a while. As I got older and faced different challenges and situations, new guides made themselves known to me, as happened recently with Pietkela.

This is typical for most, if not all, relationships between humans and guides. While most of a human's guides will be with that person for their entire lifetime, and possibly for multiple lifetimes, occasionally a guide will connect and work with a human for only part of the human's lifetime. A guide might come to assist the person with something that only lasts temporarily, like schoolwork or a home situation that ends when the person is able to leave.

As the person gets older, new guides might connect to support them through new situations that arise, such as a job or becoming a parent. As the person progresses in their spiritual growth, new guides of higher vibration might make their presence known, having been unable to work with the person previously because their vibration wasn't high enough for the connection to be safe.

One guide leaving or another showing up after a period of time doesn't mean they aren't a genuine guide or aren't actually connected with you. It simply means that any life, human or not, is an ongoing process of change and growth, and the guides who work with you might change, leave, or arrive as your life changes. Just as a kindergarten teacher might not be useful in teaching you college calculus, a guide whose main role in your life is assisting you with secondary school academics might not be able to help you become an effective parent.

Permeable vs. Impermeable

When a human connects with their guides, the connection will be either permeable or impermeable.

Permeable means that other beings in addition to the human's true guides can speak with and even connect with that person. This can be a risk, because entities that don't have the human's best interests in mind might connect with and speak to them.

In general, the person's guides will try to protect them from this, but if an entity's vibration is stronger than that of the guides, or if a being of higher vibration than the guides chooses to speak with the human, the guides might not be able to do anything about it. And if the human wants the connection and communication, whether consciously or not, their guides won't actively prevent it because doing so would violate the human's free will. The guides might advise against it, but they won't stop it.

An impermeable connection, on the other hand, means that only the person's true guides can speak with them unless explicit consent is given otherwise. Beings and entities can't just randomly show up and speak or connect with the person. They can show up and ask permission to speak with the person, but even if permission is given, they won't be able to connect, only to communicate. Often, both the human and their primary guide will have to give permission for this, since the human's free will is paramount but the primary guide will have to relax the protections they've put in place.

Because I was so young when I connected with my guides, Shiva took action to make the connection impermeable. I have had conversations with other beings, as well as with at least one malevolent entity, and with several dead spirits since one of my gifts is to act as a psychopomp (one who helps spirits cross over after death). But those conversations only happen after I and Shiva have given consent, and Shiva has closely monitored the contact to make sure I'm not in danger.

As a child, I didn't give conscious consent to having an impermeable channel or to having other communication approved and monitored by my guides, because I was too young to understand. However, on a soul level before incarnation, I had agreed to the impermeability and monitoring, and since learning more about channeling and connection I have given explicit consent.

Because having an impermeable connection means only your own guides can connect with you, impermeable channels rarely work with collectives. We can sometimes receive messages from collectives if we choose to have that ability, but a collective can't connect with and work with us on an ongoing basis generally.

The exception would be if a being who is part of a collective also chooses to act on an individual basis as a human's guide. This isn't a common occurrence; most of the time, the beings in a collective will only interact with humans as part of that collective. But it does happen.

Pietkela is an example of this. Some of the messages he conveys to me are on behalf of his collective, which in speaking with me he calls The Collaboration. But the other beings in that collective don't speak with me, and I don't receive messages from the collective as a whole. At other times, the information and messages I receive from Pietkela come from him alone. He as an individual is connected with me through the impermeable connection established by Shiva; the rest of the collective is not.

When a human connects with their guides by chance, their guide of highest vibration may or may not make the connection impermeable. It depends on factors such as the human's age, whether there's a soul-level agreement about permeability versus impermeability, and whether there are other beings or entities who are around the human and might present a danger if the connection is permeable.

At some point, if the human reaches an understanding of what's going on and that they are working with their guides, they can request a change in the structure of their connection if they choose, asking that a permeable connection be made impermeable or the other way around. (Some of the research I did for this book indicates that once a connection is made impermeable, it cannot be changed; Shiva states otherwise.)

When a human connects by choice, they are, hopefully, already aware of what's being done and who their guides are. During this process, the human can choose whether they want the connection to be permeable or impermeable, or they can ask their highest-vibration guide to make the choice that's in their highest benefit. Generally, when connection is made by choice and the human is able to understand the options, the guide won't make the decision between permeable and impermeable unless the human asks them to.

To Sum Up...

The connection and relationship between a human

and a guide can be incredibly loving and beneficial on both sides. You might think of your guides as teachers, or as friends, or even feel closer than friends with one or more of them. No way of relating to and interacting with your guides is wrong as long as it brings no harm and is agreed to by you and the guides.

However, sometimes an entity misrepresents themself as a guide and is able to convince the human, which can lead to the human being harmed. This can happen when the connection occurs by chance, particularly if it's due to incorrect or harmful "spiritual" practices, but is more likely if a human tries to connect by choice without taking proper precautions and without the guidance and protection of a trained channel and the channel's guide. In the next chapter, I'll talk more about how to know when you're connecting with an entity as opposed to a genuine guide and some precautions to take to ensure a safe connection.

When you first learn who your guides are—or sometimes even when you first learn you have guides—you may deal with feelings of unworthiness and fear. This is even more likely to happen if you've experienced bullying, abuse, or other trauma that has left you with a poor sense of self and low view of your worth.

Even though Shiva had evidenced himself to me when I was a small child, by the time I was in my thirties, I'd almost forgotten about him. My only memory of his presence when I was a child was my "make-pretend" game of being "Jesus's" daughter. That made for some strong fears of not being good enough when I learned that I would be channeling a guide who was a being of light! These fears complicated learning to work with Shiva, and for a while channeling was even more difficult because I resisted the truth out of the incorrect belief that I wasn't "worthy."

It has taken me a lot of work to overcome those thoughts, because for me as a trauma survivor, they pervade most of my life, not only my connection with my guides. I've had to shift my thinking about myself and also about who Shiva is and how he and my other guides perceive and view me. In 2006, I reconnected with and learned to channel him; as recently as 2018, I was still having to work through "But I'm not good enough to channel him" thoughts and fears. Learning that I would begin channeling Pietkela, a being of higher vibration than Shiva who acts as my guide but also speaks on behalf of a collective, I had to work through those thoughts and fears all over again.

Conversations with Shiva and Pietkela helped put those fears to rest. They reminded me that "worth" is a human construct. To them and other beings, all beings, including human, are worthy, because that is how we were created. We wouldn't question whether the Source (God, Creator, whatever term you use) is worthy, so why would we question whether we, created as reflections of that Source, are worthy?

Pietkela also pointed out that if I wasn't capable of channeling him and was somehow unworthy to convey his messages and the messages of his collective, I wouldn't have been asked to do so. Guides will ask us to do things beyond our comfort, but they won't ask us to do anything that's genuinely beyond our capabilities. Your guides, whomever they are and however high their vibration is, would not be with you if you weren't worthy of them.

Guides don't judge us. They don't measure our worth. They simply love and show compassion to us. And our connections and work with them will only be better when we learn to do the same for ourselves.

How Do You Know You're Ready to Connect with Your Guides?

- You believe your guides are there
- You're consciously aware of your guides' presence
- You're clear about your reasons for wanting to connect, and those reasons involve bringing benefit to yourself and others rather than gaining power and praise
- You're on and progressing in a path that improves your life, such as a healing journey, spiritual practice, healthier eating and exercise, etc.
- You feel a strong call to connect with them
- You make your own decisions about your life and take responsibility for your choices and actions
- You're willing to trust your guides and keep an open mind
- You're excited about the idea of connecting with your guides, even if you're also a little nervous
- You have access to a trained channel, or to books or other materials produced by a trained channel, to help ensure a safe and effective connection process
- You feel ready

A Few Words from Shiva

The connection between a guide and human is sacrosanct. Other beings will not intentionally disrupt or interfere with it. The exception comes from beings or entities with malevolent intent. Some of these entities may choose to come between a guide and human in order to corrupt the human, to cause them to take negative or harmful actions. At times, there may be a history between the guide and the entity, and this is the cause of the entity's choice to interfere, but this is rare.

When a guide connects to a human, if the human so chooses, that connection may be made what is called "impermeable." This means that only those beings who are intended to work with that human as guides may communicate with and connect to that human. Exceptions may be made for other beings at the human's request, or sometimes at the request of the beings, for there are instances when a human might benefit from communication with a being who is not among their guides, but the human cannot request this communication because they are unaware that the being exists.

At times, a guide may form the initial connection with the human when the human is a young child. This is often the result of trauma; unable to find succor or safety from the adult humans around them, the child in their pain cries out to the Universe for aid. This can have the unfortunate side effect of drawing entities rather than the child's true guides, particularly if the entities have a more powerful energetic vibration than the guides. However, this is uncommon.

In general, when a child cries out at these times, the call is answered by one of their true guides, often the guide of highest vibration. At this time, the guide will "cap the channel," so to speak, rendering the child impermeable so that even should they continue to cry out, only their own guides will answer the call. This creates safety for the child, and also enables their guides to speak with them more regularly and more clearly to try to aid them in protecting themself or to assist them in finding aid amongst other humans.

When a child connects with their guides, they often consider their guides to be "imaginary friends." Should they speak of their guides to others, those others will often insist that the guides are imaginary. However, it is easy to tell the difference between a guide and a genuine imaginary friend. When the child is communicating with a figment of their imagination, that figment can only know what the child knows. When the child is communicating with their guides, the guides have access to far more knowledge and understanding than does the child, and therefore are able to give the child guidance and information the child could not create themself.

Guides who choose to work with humans have a variety of levels of energetic vibration. However, a guide's vibration will always be higher than that of the human with whom they're working. This is because the act of incarnating in and of itself lowers energetic vibration, as do experiences through which humans go throughout their lives.

It is important to note that the names or labels of types of beings are for the convenience of humans, and are not necessarily what the beings would call themselves. For some of us, names and labels are unnecessary. For others, the term that is used would be unpronounceable or incomprehensible to humans, so it is changed or simplified.

When a human connects with their guide, the guide comes to them without gender, without name, without label. Although the guide will be a specific type of being, that type, as stated, may not be labeled as a human would label it, or may have a name or designation humans are unable to use.

Likewise, gender is not something experienced by beings. Even human souls, when not incarnate, are not gendered. Beings will often, however, choose to present themselves as a gender with which the human will be comfortable. I, for example, present myself as male to my host Ganatram, for they are more comfortable with males than with any other gender. However, in my true form, in my true being, I have no gender; the choice to present as male was made solely for the comfort and ease of my host.

Names are also chosen for the comfort and convenience of the human, for humans require names and labels to make sense of things. A guide may choose a name by which other humans have known them, for some guides work with multiple humans over the course of their existence, or they may choose a name they detect in the human's mind.

When I began work with my Ganatram, they were very young and did not comprehend many names. As they attended church with their parent, and were familiar with the name Jesus, for a time that name was what they called me. When they grew older, I offered them other names, until they and I began to work together more fully and the channel who facilitated our connection offered them the name "Shiva" by which to know me. However, that name is not mine any more than the name "Jesus" or any other name by which Ganatram or other humans have known me. I am what humans call a being of light, and have no need of name or designation in my natural existence; however, in my work with humans, a name is needed.

Sometimes, a guide may push the boundaries of the human's comfort by choosing to remain nameless or by helping the human comprehend a name by which the being is known (for those beings who have names in their natural existence). They may push the human's "comfort zone," so to speak, by declining to present as any gender. These decisions are made based upon the guide's understanding of what the human wants and needs to learn from them, and are not made to force the human to accept something or to cause the human extreme *discomfort.*

Although the human may not be fully conscious of what they need to learn in order to progress in their growth and journey, the guide is aware, for the guide has access to greater knowledge than does the human, and the guide is able to see into the human's subconscious as well as see beyond the human themself to the broader range of decisions and choices made at the soul level.

When connecting with a guide, it is acceptable to request a name and a gender if the guide does not offer one when introducing themself. However, know that you may not receive the answer you seek, or may receive a different answer, or receive the answer in a different way, than you anticipate.

When working with your guides, you need not fear that they will abandon or judge you. You need not fear our anger or hatred, for these are not things we experience. The only humanlike emotion experienced by the beings who work for the benefit of humans is love. Whatever you choose, whether you accept or reject our guidance—or indeed, whether you accept or reject us—you are loved by your guides, by the beings who observe and work with broader ranges of humans, and by the Creative Power of the Universe itself. Love informs all that a guide does, and is the most prominent gift we offer to you.

6 Good, Bad, or Other: How to Know

The Power of Free Will

We humans have the ability to choose our spiritual connections and the power to discern whether beings and entities are benevolent, malevolent, or neutral. Some people, though, are unaware they possess this ability or don't trust their own intuition. They assume if a being comes to them, they have to work with that being even if they don't want to or feel uncomfortable, and that they have to listen to whatever the being tells them.

The most important thing to know when working with beings is that a true guide will advise you without interfering with your free will or autonomy. Connections with guides are meant to help you live your life, not tell you how to live or force you to do things in a certain way. Even if you make decisions which aren't in your best interest, a true guide won't prevent you from making them. They will advise you against them and help you see the potential consequences, but the final decision is entirely up to you.

In connecting and working with true guides, control over the interactions lies with the human. Free will is paramount. Even when a guide chooses to work with a human, it can only happen if the human also chooses it. Since not all humans are aware they have guides, this choice might not be made on a conscious level. It may come from the subconscious or might have been made at the soul level prior to incarnation. But it's still a choice, and you can always change your mind. You choose whether and how to interact with your guides and even whether to accept them as your guides.

You're never obligated to listen to what your guides say, and many true guides will tell you this. If they say something that's uncomfortable for you to hear, it might be a sign that you need to push your comfort zone and do some growing and changing rather than a lack of truth in their words. If you simply feel like what they've told you is "too scary" or "too hard" to do, that doesn't mean you shouldn't listen. But if something genuinely doesn't resonate or feel true to you, you don't have to go along with it just because it's coming from a guide. A guide won't be offended or upset that you aren't listening to them, because they are invested in maintaining your free will.

They Aren't All Good Guys

Not all beings are benevolent. As I said in a previous chapter, I refer to the benevolent ones as beings and the malevolent ones as entities, and I'll be using those terms here as well.

It's vital to know who you're working with when you connect and channel. This is why I strongly recommend only working with a trained channel if you're connecting by choice. A trained channel and their guide can help protect you from entities who are attracted to you and want to cause trouble. A channel's guide will be able to communicate with your guides on a different level and ensure that the only beings that come through to connect and speak with you are your true guides.

If you connect on your own by choice or chance, it's a bit more difficult to ensure the same level of safety. If you choose to on your own, I recommend using a resource such as a book or meditation created by a trained channel. Often in these resources, the channel's guide invites people to call on them for assistance in the connection process, and I advise doing so if it's an option. You can also set sacred space, if that's part of your spiritual belief system, in which to attempt the connection, and you can ask that a being you've worked with previously, such as an angel or deity from your spiritual path, be present to protect you.

Although a malevolent entity will try to trick you into believing they're your true guide, there are certain traits and qualities that will give them away. No matter how careful they are to keep up the façade, it's nearly impossible for them to hide their true nature for long.

If nothing else, the way you feel when interacting with them will give them away. An entity will leave you feeling drained and depleted, and you may have a visceral negative reaction to their presence, including possibly being physically ill.

A low-level or malevolent entity will often predict disasters and give specific details about the future. These disasters may or may not come to pass, and specific details about any future interfere with the human's free will by pushing them toward a certain course of action. The entity may also stroke your ego by saying things like,

"This awful thing will happen, but your vibration is so high it won't affect you and you should feel sorry for the people with lower vibrations."

Alternatively, the entity might diminish your ego through insults and demeaning talk. One friend of mine had a negative entity pretending to be a guide and constantly heard things like "You're so stupid, why won't you listen to me?" and "You'll never get anywhere if you don't do what I say, because you're too incompetent." My friend was also threatened with physical harm if they didn't listen to the entity. These are not things a genuine guide would ever say to the human they're working with! If you're receiving threats, insults, and demeaning talk, you are not speaking to a true guide.

Entities might also suggest or encourage courses of actions that will harm you or others. The friend I mention above was told by the entity to engage in self-harming behavior and to "get revenge" on people who had hurt them. An entity might also push you into conflict with other people to separate you from those who love you so you have to rely on the entity.

In some ways, a connection with a malevolent entity is very similar to an abusive relationship with another human. And just as it can be hard to recognize someone as abusive in the early stages of a relationship and can be complicated to leave them even when you realize they're abusing you, recognizing an entity as malevolent and separating yourself from them isn't always easy. But you can learn to distinguish your genuine guides from entities, and you have the power to end a connection with an entity when you choose to do so.

If you're connected with or interact with a low-level entity, each interaction will leave you feeling drained and depressed. You may experience feelings of hopelessness and powerlessness, and you'll begin to doubt yourself and your perceptions. But you may also have "delusions of grandeur" in which you believe you're better than everyone else and are more "advanced," because this is what the entity tells you.

While a true guide will encourage you and try to help you build your confidence, they won't tell you that you're superior to anyone else. And while the energy shifts as your guide comes and goes might leave you feeling tired, revved-up, or just "off," you won't feel drained or negative about the interaction.

Some beings and entities are neither benevolent nor malevolent. They're very different from us and noticeably not human. They don't experience emotions and may not even experience love and compassion even though those are constants throughout much of the Universe. Most beings of this type aren't interested in humans at all and won't interact with us. However, some are a little curious about us, and they'll respond if they feel a human has called on them.

These beings won't deliberately cause trouble or give false information. However, because they are very much distanced from humans, a person who deals with one of these beings may feel uncomfortable or struggle to communicate with them. These beings and entities are unlikely to cause you harm, at least not intentionally, but the information they convey is also not likely to benefit you.

Trust Yourself to Know the Difference

Trust how you feel when a being is present. A high-level being or true guide is with you to offer guidance, support, and compassion. They want to help you attain your highest good, and won't try to scare or flatter you. These beings encourage you to tap into your own wisdom, even if it leads you to disagree with them or reject what they say. They know their truth isn't the only truth, and they readily acknowledge this.

A true guide generally won't give predictions of the future. Although they might sometimes indicate possible outcomes, what they tell you won't be specific. If you want to know whether you're going to get a particular job, a guide probably won't tell you. If you want to know whether your job situation will change, the guide might be willing to answer that, because it's more general.

Specific or detailed answers about the future cause issues with the person's free will, because if a human believes they know what's going to happen, they might not take the actions they need to take that would actually lead to that outcome.

When you receive a message from a true guide, whether it's your own guide or during a session with a trained channel, the guide will be completely honest. Guides do not lie. In fact, Shiva has told me that the beings who act as guides, and most benevolent beings that interact with humans, are generally unable to lie. They also won't intentionally mislead. If they're unable to tell you something, they'll say so; they won't make up an answer or say something they don't know to be true.

However, this honesty means you might not always like what you hear. Guides will convey their messages as compassionately as possible, but they will tell you what they believe you need to know. Humans don't always like hearing what's true; the saying "the truth hurts" exists for a reason. But a guide is telling you what they believe you need to know to help you understand the changes and growth you need in your life. We don't always like hearing that we need to change, but there's a difference between being harmed by what you hear and being uncomfortable with or disliking the message.

A true guide won't present their messages in a hurtful or malicious way. They aren't judging you or trying to make you feel bad. They're simply pointing out something about your life that isn't benefiting you. They also won't share anything against your free will or that you aren't ready to hear and address, but again, that doesn't always mean you're going to like what they say. It's important to be able to distinguish between an entity giving harmful or incorrect information and a true guide whose message is something to which your ego is resistant.

Depending on what a guide tells you, you may not feel ready to hear it or consciously might not want to hear it. However, guides operate from a place of knowing what your subconscious and unconscious mind want and need as well as your conscious mind. If you're truly unready, or if the information is incorrect, they won't give it. If it's only your conscious mind or ego that feel unready or unwilling to accept the message while your subconscious is ready, they'll share it anyway. It's still your choice whether to listen and accept it.

Even if you don't like what a true guide tells you, your emotions and intuition can help you recognize whether they're who they claim to be. After working with a true guide, you'll feel supported, heard, and uplifted. Maybe not comfortable, and maybe not altogether happy with what you've been told, but in general you will have a calm and even positive sense. Some fear might arise because your ego fears the actions you'll need to take, but if you're actually frightened of the *being* or feel bullied by them, they are probably not a true guide.

Guidance Is All About You

Genuine guides won't give you information about other people or what they should do. A true guide offers insight that focuses on *you*: your inner power, your responsibility, and the things over which you actually have control.

At one point, Shiva and I did a trance channeling for someone who was having issues with their child, who had reached adulthood and wasn't living the life the parent wanted them to live. The parent asked questions like, "Why isn't my child doing this?" and "How can I help them to live the life I think is best for them?"

Shiva outright refused to answer a couple of those questions. With the ones he was willing to answer, his responses included, "Why do you believe your child should live their life the way you want rather than the way they want?" and "Perhaps you would receive more useful guidance were you to ask how you can communicate more effectively with your child rather than focusing upon what they are and are not doing."

Our client wasn't altogether pleased with those answers, but told me later that on reflection, they understood that Shiva was respecting their child's free will and was also trying to help them see that rather than actually helping, they were unintentionally trying to control their child.

Whether you're speaking with your own guide or having a session with a trained channel, you're unlikely to get answers about another person. Guides respect free will, and giving you information about someone who isn't present to consent to that information being shared would violate that person's free will. Likewise, telling you how to "make" the person do what you think they should do violates the person's free will.

I always recommend that when having a channeling session or speaking with your own guides, you ask questions about your own role in someone's life instead of about the other person. For example, instead of "Why isn't my teenager doing their homework?" a better question, and one a guide might be more willing to answer, might be, "How can I help my teenager become more cooperative about doing their homework?"

It can be much easier for humans to examine what we think someone else needs to do or change than to hear what *we* need to do or change, but guides aren't interested in taking the easy path. They're here to help us learn and grow, and that includes taking a look—sometimes a painful one—at what we're doing that contributes to issues between us and others rather than letting us focus on what the others are doing.

Channeling vs. Possession

Sometimes when I talk to people about channeling, they assume it's the same as possession. One person even told me that he knows people whose guides "force them" (his words) to let the guides speak through them even if they don't want to allow it.

That is absolutely not the behavior of a genuine guide. That is possession, not channeling. A true guide will never force anything on a human.

Possession is when an entity takes over a human's body against the human's will. This is almost always done by malevolent entities, and often they stay within the human's consciousness, energy system, and body even when the human doesn't want them there and when the entity isn't actively doing anything. Unfortunately, after a while of this, the human becomes accustomed to and sometimes even likes what the entity does. They then have no interest in ending the possession, which is exactly what the entity hopes for.

By contrast, when I channel, even during trance channeling, it is entirely by my choice. Shiva and Pietkela do sometimes approach me and say, "I have a message I'd like you to share," but I can refuse to write or speak the message, or I can say "not now, how about this afternoon," or whatever I choose. They won't "knock me out" of my body to allow them to speak or write through me if I'm unwilling to do the channeling. They wait until I'm willing.

If I agree to convey the message, we discuss how I'll do so, and this again is my choice. For general messages, I most often type them and share them on social media or in another venue, but I may agree to do a video. Once we've decided on the how, we discuss whether I'll be doing relayed or trance channeling.

If we agree on trance, I have to go through my trance induction process and then explicitly invite my guide to enter my body and speak or type through me. Even if I go through the induction process and am fully in trance, neither Shiva nor Pietkela will "come in" until they're invited. They could; they have the energetic vibration and the power to do so. But they won't, because my free will is paramount.

Some people may make agreements with their guides that allow their guides to speak through them whenever the guides choose, and that's fine. It's a decision that is specific to each pair of human and guide. But that agreement still indicates the human's choice and free will, even if it's a "blanket" thing and not explicitly given each time. A genuine guide will not violate a human's free will under any circumstances, including having the human convey a message from the guide, no matter how important the message may be.

To Sum Up...

True guides also won't advise any course of action that's potentially harmful to you or someone else. They encourage you to care for yourself and to find nonviolent ways of managing situations, and to continue your learning and growth even when you feel like withdrawing or giving up. A genuine guide will encourage a human to seek the human's highest ideal even when it's uncomfortable or difficult, and they'll be there to support you in the work.

My guides have literally kept me alive at times; because of the trauma I've experienced plus clinical mental illness, there have been a number of times in my life when I've wanted to end everything, and a very few times when I've actually tried. Every time, my guides were with me, talking to me, reminding me that I'm loved. Any time I tell them I'm in that mindset, they respond the same way.

If a guide—or what you believe to be a guide—tells you to hurt yourself, encourages revenge on others, or suggests any other course of action that might cause harm to you or anyone else, they are not a guide. If they force you to channel them, insult you or others, or stroke your ego and tell you you're superior, they are not a guide. This is the behavior of a malevolent entity. Our guides want the best for us and for all humans; they have no reason to advise anything destructive, look down on us, or encourage us to look down on others.

How Do You Know a Guide Is Genuine?

- They speak kindly even if they're disagreeing with you
- They're honest with you even if you don't necessarily like what you hear
- They advise courses of action that are nonharmful and don't interfere with your well-being or other people
- They encourage you to make your own decisions and listen to your own intuition about whether the things you hear are true
- They help build your confidence without stroking your ego
- They offer suggestions and advice but leave the final decisions up to you
- They ask your consent before connecting with you or delivering information
- They encourage you to accept responsibility for your life and choices and to embrace your inner power to create the life you want
- They speak to you as an equal collaborator, not someone inferior
- They admit they don't know everything
- You feel positive, uplifted, and supported when interacting with them, even if the energy shifts also cause discomfort or fatigue. (It's normal for energy shifts to do this regardless of whether a being is a true guide.)

A Few Words from Shiva

Malevolent entities that communicate with humans do not do so for the benefit of any save themselves. They do so in order to cause pain and struggle, or at times because they know no better or do not have the perception to comprehend that their actions may cause harm to the humans. I use "entity" for those discorporate consciousnesses who wish to cause harm, and "being" for those who wish to bring benefit solely for the purpose of distinguishing between the two; in actuality, either term is correct for either type.

If a being feels to you as if its vibration is lower than yours, this is not a true guide and may be detrimental to you; it will be best to remove it from you. This may be done simply by requesting that it leave, or by taking stronger measures such as seeking assistance from a human who is trained in working with guides or from your true guides, who will come and assist you if asked but are unable to do so if you do not ask, for they cannot act against your free will. Again, exceptions are made when the human is a young child who is not yet capable of comprehending what is occurring.

There are entities who mean harm to humans or who will not bring benefit, yet whose energetic vibrations still are higher than humans. In this case, you will not feel that they are low vibration. However, you may feel discomfort in their presence, for your instincts and intuition will attempt to alert you when you are dealing with an entity who does not have benevolent intent.

These entities may also give away their true nature through things such as speaking negatively or angrily toward you. Calling names, expressing anger, insulting you, or advising you to do things which might bring harm to you or others are not the actions of a true guide, but of an entity with malevolent intent. If your "guide's" words and instructions cause you to feel hurt, frightened, or excessively angry, be aware that this is unlikely to truly be one of your guides, and take the steps to remove them from you as mentioned earlier.

The anger to which I refer is not the same as anger you might feel when a true guide advises you in a course of action you do not wish to take. It is human nature to feel anger and fear when confronted with uncomfortable truths. If your guide states something which you know to be true or to be a beneficial course of action, and you feel anger in response, this is not an indication that you are not interacting with your true guide, but rather of the fact that you are human and your ego seeks to prevent change at all costs.

Anger felt when confronted with truth is ego-based; anger felt when an entity speaks to you negatively or causes harm is based upon the mind's need for protection. The distinction is difficult to put into words, but you may trust how you feel at these times, for the difference will be apparent to you in the situation.

If you become aware that an entity whom you trusted as a guide is in actuality harmful to you, you may request that it leave you. At times, this is sufficient, for part of the entity's purpose is to obscure their true self from you. When it becomes aware that you have recognized it for what it is, it may choose to leave on its own or will leave when asked to do so. If this is unsuccessful, seek assistance in separating the entity from you. There are among you humans who are trained in this, who can aid you. You may also ask that your true guides step forward to assist, and they will do so; be aware, however, that at times an entity may have a higher energetic vibration than your own guides, and seeking assistance from another source will be necessary.

You may also reach out to beings such as myself, for even if we are not your guides and do not work directly with you, we wish to assist humans in achieving growth and progress in their spiritual lives, and we wish to protect you from those who may harm or hinder you. I am called Shiva; if you require aid in removing an entity from *you, you may call upon me.*

7 Honesty, Ethics, Consent, and Trust

When You Work With Your Guides

As with almost anything in life, when it comes to connecting with and channeling your guides, there are some reasons that are less positive and beneficial than others.

The connection with your guides is intended to help you grow and learn spiritually. To progress in your life and to bring benefit to yourself and other people. It isn't so you can brag about who your guides are or about being able to talk to them. Bragging comes from your ego, the part of you that wants to be better than everyone else while simultaneously believing you'll never be good enough. It's one of the things your guides may wish to help you learn not to do.

Always be honest when working with your guides. They won't be dishonest with you. If you're dishonest with them, they're likely to be aware of it and may call you on it, though they'll do so in as gentle a way as possible. They aren't interested in making you feel bad. They simply want you to be accountable for and honest about your choices.

Your guides don't want to live your life for you, nor do they want to constantly tell you how to live your life. Your life is meant to be your own creation. Guides will advise you on what actions and decisions might be most beneficial, but they won't tell you which choices to make.

If you're looking for someone to walk alongside you as you progress on your life's path, that's what you'll have with your guides. But if you're looking for someone to carry you along that path and take the responsibility for your choices, your guides aren't going to give you that. Learning to create our lives and take responsibility for what we choose is part of every human's life path, and guides won't take those lessons away from us.

When you're connected with your guides, if you find yourself constantly asking them what you should do or waiting for them to advise you before doing anything, or turn to them at times when you already know the choice you want to make but don't trust yourself, they might pull back. They won't leave, because guides don't abandon us, but they may start refusing to answer your questions or be firmer about helping you find your own answers instead of just giving you information.

Guides want to help us become more autonomous and take more ownership of our lives. We each have the power to own our lives and choices. The relationship with our guides is intended to be a collaboration between equally independent beings.

When You Tell Others About Your Guides

While some people choose to work with their guides only in their own lives, some choose to become channels who share their guides' wisdom and messages with others.

Most of the time, a channel will work with their primary guide or guide of highest vibration to do this. This is a valid path, but channeling for others requires additional considerations to make sure you're doing so in an ethical manner.

Your guides' primary role is to help *you* progress in your life's path. This path might include channeling for others if you and your guides agree to it, but that doesn't mean the guide you channel will randomly give you information about other people. Nor is it acceptable to ask them to. Channeling for others isn't an excuse to intrude on people's privacy.

At times if you're talking to someone else, your guide might give you information to share with that person. This usually indicates that either something the other person has said shows willingness and need to hear what your guide has to say, or your guide has connected with that person's guide and received their consent to offer the message. A genuine guide won't just say "Tell them this" out of the blue.

When it comes to sharing messages from your guides, refrain from just blurting it out. Not everyone believes in guides, and not everyone who believes in them wants to hear what someone else's guide has to say. You have the right and power to choose whether to listen to your guides, and you need to give other people the same right and power to choose whether to hear what you want to pass along from your guides. Ask someone's consent before passing along something your guide has said.

In the first chapter, I mentioned my "accidental" visit to a metaphysical shop in Florida, where I learned from the store owner that I would begin working with a guide other than Shiva. The owner didn't give me that information spontaneously or without obtaining my consent. We struck up a conversation and talked about a few related topics, until I mentioned that I did channeling. Then the owner chuckled a bit and started to say something. She stopped herself and instead said, "May I tell you what my guides are telling me about that?"

I thanked her for asking first and agreed to hear what her guides had to say. That was when she told me I would begin channeling a being other than Shiva, along with some other pieces of information that were more personal.

She made an ethical choice. Instead of just saying what her guides were saying to her, she asked whether I wanted to hear it.

Some people might be willing to hear what you and your guides have to say but might question it or want confirmation. That isn't anything personal against you. My guides, and other guides I've had experience with, always advise humans to use their discernment and trust their instincts above all else. That doesn't mean don't trust others; it means it's okay to double check if you aren't certain about something. It also means it's okay for others to double check what you and your guides say to them if they're unsure about it.

When the store owner told me that I would be working with a different guide, as I said in a previous chapter, some of the things she said felt to me like she was stroking my ego, even though they also felt true. I know I sometimes tend to let my ego get the better of me, so on my way home, I asked Shiva to confirm what she'd said. I needed to be sure not only that she was speaking the full truth, but also that I wasn't letting a desire for praise and "specialness" cloud my perception.

Shiva did confirm what the owner had told me, and informed me that the being the owner referenced was

Pietkela, a being with whom I'd already been communicating even though I hadn't known he was one of my guides. Wanting his reassurance wasn't due to distrusting the store owner or even distrusting myself. It was a matter of wanting to consider everything that might prevent me from seeing the most beneficial course of action. I believed the owner, and having Shiva's confirmation enabled me to trust the situation enough to take the next steps on my path.

Each person has a right to determine whether something feels true and right for them, and everyone has a responsibility to use and trust their intuition and discernment. If someone wants confirmation or a second opinion, they aren't calling you a liar or saying they don't believe you. They're simply exercising that right and responsibility.

In addition to consent, honesty is vital when talking about your guide to or sharing their messages with others. Strive to be as accurate and honest as possible. Your guide gives you the truth as they perceive it, and if you're called to pass that truth along to others, it's best to use your guide's words.

When you channel for someone else, you can do so by relayed channeling, in which your guide tells you what they want to say and you pass it along to the other person, or trance channeling, in which you enter a trance state and allow your guide to speak directly through you. Trance channeling makes honesty and accuracy a bit easier; your guide is speaking, so there's no chance of you misinterpreting or deliberately changing their words.

However, in relayed channeling, there's sometimes a temptation to alter the message. You might consider censoring what your guides say so the other person won't get upset, or changing the message in other ways because you want to make sure they listen and believe you. Neither of these is okay.

While your guides bear responsibility for their words, and you bear responsibility for yours, changing the words because of the risk of upsetting someone else isn't beneficial and may be dishonest. Instead, deliver the message in the kindest way you can without changing the words, or add your own words afterward to offer support and compassion.

Your guides know what the other person needs to hear and will give you their messages in nonharmful, compassionate language. The other person has full free will as to whether to listen to the information, and it isn't anything personal against you or your guides if they choose not to listen. You don't need to change anything your guides say.

You also don't have anything to prove to anyone. There's no need to change your guide's messages or say your guide has said something they haven't actually said just to try to convince another person that you're really speaking with your guides. It isn't up to you to convince them, and being dishonest about who your guides are or what they've said will have the opposite effect from what you want. Using your guides as leverage to persuade someone to do what you say or that your words are valid is another way your ego might trip you up, and it's unethical.

Being a channel, or a reader, psychic, medium, or any other type of metaphysical or spiritual practitioner, does not give you the right to drop information and messages on people at random. They may not want to hear it, or may not be ready for it. And it's pretty rude to go up to a stranger in a store, for example, and tell them you have a message for them!

Always ask consent. Just as your guides need and ask for your consent before connecting and speaking with you, and just as your consent is required for channeling, you need to ask for other people's consent before sharing what you channel. If it's a general message that you're, say, sharing on Facebook, you don't need to ask everyone's consent; it's fair to presume that if they're reading your post, they're consenting to hearing the message. But if it's something you feel called to share with an individual or that you think is relevant to them, ask if it's okay first. And if they say no, accept that.

No is a complete sentence, regardless of whether we're talking about channeling or anything else in life. It isn't an invitation to argue or persuade or demand justification. Accept that the person isn't willing to hear what you want to say, and move on.

Just as there's a risk that you might become too dependent on your guides, when you choose to share your guides' messages with other people, there's a risk that those people will become too dependent on you. They might constantly turn to you for advice or to get more information from your guides.

This is a risk to their autonomy and ability to take responsibility for their lives, but it's also a risk for you. Having someone treat you like an authority and regularly ask you to help them figure out their lives can be one heck of an ego boost, and it's easy to get sucked into the hype. If you offer your guides' guidance to others, be mindful of how it feels for you. Are you doing it to be of service to those people? Or is part of you doing it to receive praise and accolades?

Avoid letting others become dependent on you and your guides' messages. If you choose to channel for others, do so because you want to help and serve them, not to gain followers or have them listen to you above their own knowledge and intuition. Also avoid relying on other people for validation and acceptance of your connection with your guides or of your gifts and skills. If it seems that someone is leaning on you too much, or you feel yourself needing to have other people listen to and validate you, it might be best to pull back from them, at least temporarily.

To Sum Up...

Guides are with us to help us progress in our spiritual paths and our life journeys. They aren't here to tell us what to do, and it's important not to become so dependent on them that we stop making our own decisions. Similarly, if we channel for others, we need to make sure they don't become reliant on us and our guides. While it might feel good to the ego to have someone constantly turning to us for advice and guidance, it doesn't benefit anyone.

If we're becoming too dependent on our guides, they may stop giving us their input or even stop speaking with us altogether for a little while, though not without warning. If we realize someone else is turning to us for guidance too often, we have the ethical responsibility to stop providing channeling for them until they've learned that they have the power to make their own choices.

More importantly, when working with our guides for ourselves or channeling them for others, we need to do so in an ethical way. If we have a message for someone else, we need to ask their consent before blurting it out. Bragging about who our guide is or about having the skill isn't ethical. It's ego, and it can place us in a position where either people think we have authority we don't have or where people are unwilling to listen to us because we've shown ourselves as someone who wants to be "superior." Saying you can channel and naming your guide is fine. It's only a problem when you brag about it or use it to try to position yourself in a place of superiority.

When we share what our guides tell us, we need to be as accurate and honest as possible about what they said. Changing or censoring their words, even if we think it's for the client's benefit, is dishonest and doesn't serve the other person. Further, it can cause loss of trust between that person and us, or between us and our guides.

Ultimately, the connection between a human and a guide is a bond of mutual love, respect, learning, and growth. Guides don't consider themselves "above" or "better than" humans, merely different, and they approach us as equals and friends. When we work with them at that level, the benefits are immeasurable.

How Do You Know If You're Acting Ethically?

- You take responsibility for your actions and their consequences
- You avoid becoming dependent on others for your decisions and choices, including your guides
- You speak honestly and authentically but with kindness and compassion
- You discourage others from becoming dependent on you for their decisions and choices
- You ask consent before giving someone channeled messages, healing energy, or anything of that kind.
- You refrain from positioning yourself as superior
- You respect free will—others and your own
- You're concerned about being ethical and continually work to ensure you behave ethically

I would like to note that ethics are somewhat

subjective. The above list is intended as general guidelines. Asking consent, being honest without being deliberately hurtful, and not placing yourself in a position of superiority over anyone else are ethical ways of behaving no matter who you are or what context you're acting in. Your personal code of ethics may vary.

The basic foundation of any ethical practice is harming none; as long as you start from that principle, you are likely to act in an ethical manner.

A Few Words from Shiva

In all of our interactions with humans, we, your guides and beings who interact with you, endeavor to observe free will. Although our codes of morals and ethics may differ from yours in some ways, the concepts of autonomy, responsibility, consent, and honesty are consistent.

We have no wish to interfere with choices you may make. Although we may advise you against certain courses of actions and encourage others, we will not speak in terms of "musts" and "have tos," but rather in terms of "do you feel this will benefit you" or "is this truly the most beneficial choice?"

In our work with you, we seek our own spiritual growth but also wish to facilitate yours. One cannot grow spiritually without learning to make their own decisions and accept responsibility and accountability for them.

We will never lie or seek to mislead you. Indeed, for some of us, lying is impossible or simply is not something which would occur to us. Likewise, we will never encourage you to be dishonest with another, excepting, perhaps, situations in which the truth would endanger you. Even then, we will encourage and attempt to aid you in finding a safe way to speak the truth.

We will not hide information from you intentionally, though at times we may express that we are unable to relay certain things. This is not to hide or obscure anything from you, but rather to observe your free will. When this occurs, the information has been deemed not to be beneficial to you or would interfere with your ability to freely choose your course, or you do not wish to hear it or are not yet ready for it. We will not speak to you of things which you are unready to accept, even if that lack of readiness is not on a conscious level.

When we speak with you, when we work with you in ways other than speech, when you channel us for others, we do so only with consent. When my Ganatram channels me in trance, they must explicitly invite me to place my consciousness in their physical form. If they do not issue this invitation, I will not enter. At times, I ask or encourage them to channel something from me; however, they always have the option to say no, and I respect and abide by that decision.

We wish you to know that even when you hold wisdom or knowledge that you believe is of benefit, it is unethical to force that upon others. You may have a "message" for another, but it compromises their free will and their right to consent if you simply walk up to them and speak the message. We do not negate or deny your free will and autonomy; we ask that you have the same consideration for one another.

Additionally, when you choose to channel for others, or to share with them other wisdom you possess, we encourage you to remember that you are not superior to them. In my introduction to this book, I stated that despite being a being of light, I am not superior to humans, merely different. This is the case with each of you as well.

You possess skills others lack. You hold gifts others do not possess. You are able to bring into the world things which no one else can bring. Yet none of this renders you superior to any other. Superiority is the province of ego, or rather of the part of your ego which desires to be better than others while believing itself to be nothing.

You are not nothing, but neither are you better than others. The world, indeed the Universe, needs what you bring, but to bring the light and healing that is within your power, you must act in such a way that honors the free will, skills, and gifts others possess. There is no superior or inferior, merely different.

Because of our wish to observe your free will, we do not command certain courses of action. We advise and encourage, but the choice is always yours. Due to this, if we perceive that you are becoming overly reliant upon us to make your choices and decisions, we may pull back from you for a time so that you may regain your autonomy and independence.

Our relationships with our hosts and with other humans are not meant to be that of an authority and followers, or of parent and child, but that of collaborators in the creation of a positive life and world. Collaborators work together; one does not "pull rank," so to speak, over the other. One collaborator does not tell another what to do while the other simply waits for instruction; each works upon their own tasks and path, and speak to one another and encourage certain ideas and tasks.

Such it is when you connect and work with your guides. We are not with you to absolve you of responsibility for your life, but rather to increase your ability and willingness to take that responsibility. We wish to assist and support you, not to live your lives for you.

And we wish you to assist others rather than causing or encouraging them to rely overly much upon you.

8 Afterword

The subject of guides and beings is one often discussed in metaphysical and other circles. Most religions and spiritual paths acknowledge the existence of beings such as God or other deities, angels, and malevolent entities.

There isn't always agreement on what the beings who work with humans are called, or how much of the information they convey actually comes from them rather than coming from the egos of the humans who say they speak for the beings. There are a lot of things we don't know about guides and channeling, and while there is a scientific basis for the concepts, just as there is for things like energy healing, our science hasn't quite caught up with the less concrete things.

I don't consider myself the ultimate authority on guides. The information I've shared in this book is either what I was taught by my mentor or what I channeled from Shiva and Pietkela. Although it's in line with what I found during my research to create the book, it may disagree with other sources. I hope as you read the book, you did so with an "ear," so to speak, toward your own intuition.

Connecting with guides is something in which many people are interested, but there are safer and less safe ways to do it. As I said earlier in this book, I strongly advise either working with a trained channel and their guide to connect with your own or at least using a book written by a trained channel. This is not that book; I intentionally didn't include instruction on connecting with your guides because forming that connection is not something to do lightly. The bibliography has a few suggestions of books to use as resources if you're interested in connecting with your guides. I also offer instruction in it in collaboration with Pietkela, and I'll be releasing a book on the subject in the future.

Your guides are with you, whether or not you're consciously aware of it. They want to help you progress in your life, and they want to do so in collaboration with you rather than in authority over you. Learning about your guides and learning to work with them is a journey, as are so many things in life; even as I was writing the first draft of this book, I was learning more and understanding more about my guides and the work we may do together.

The first step in working with your guides is accepting that they're there and that you deserve their love, compassion, and support. I hope this book has helped you in taking that first step.

9 A Few Closing Words from Shiva

In my existence, I have been honored to be able to connect and work with certain humans. At times, this work has consisted merely of conveying messages to them; at other times, I have become their guide and we have worked closely together to grow and learn as well as to pass knowledge and compassion to others.

The bond between a guide and a human is a loving and beneficial one on both sides. We beings who act as guides have no desire to command humans, nor do we consider ourselves superior to you. We wish only to impart our knowledge and to gain additional knowledge from you. It is a symbiosis of sorts, in which both parties learn and grow from one another.

I am equally honored to have been able to contribute to this book. Although each of you who read these words have guides with you, you may not yet be fully aware of their presence or may be uncertain of how to communicate with them. Know that your guides are truly there, and that you need only speak to them in order to be heard.

Undertaking the intentional process of connection with your guides is not a choice to make lightly, nor is it a game or trick. We are with you to assist you in your spiritual path and to progress in our own; the connection is not intended to be used to gain power nor to entertain your friends at parties. We do not expect nor request complete seriousness at all times, for your joy and humor are among the things which appeal to us the most. However, there is a difference between being humorous and playful at times and treating your connection with us as simply something to do for fun or to "show off," as you might say.

Nothing you ask of us is considered frivolous or silly so long as you ask of your own free will and for your own benefit and growth or to assist another in their growth. My Ganatram has regularly requested that I perform energy work to facilitate their physical and emotional health. Each time, they hesitate to ask, fearing they are "asking too much" or that the request is unnecessary. This is never the case; it is Ganatram's own fears and the impressions left by past experiences. For me, it is a privilege to be able to assist them in this manner, and I do not keep tallies of how frequently they ask.

Your relationship with your guides may be the same if you choose it to be. You may form a bond with them which allows you to request their assistance and their facilitation of your health and well-being. You may form a bond such as I have with my Ganatram, which includes playfulness and friendship as well as spiritual work. In relating with your guides, there is no single "right" way so long as you approach it for beneficial reasons.

In this book, we have not included instruction in connecting with your guides, for that is an undertaking which requires more direct support and instruction than could be provided in this text. It would also have detracted from the purpose of this book, which was merely to educate you about the existence of guides. In a future work, Ganatram, in collaboration with their primary guide Pietkela, will offer instruction and protection for those seeking to create or strengthen their conscious connection with their guides.

For this time, know that means do exist to create and strengthen this connection, and that it is a process best undertaken with support and guidance from a human who is trained in such matters and who works in conjunction with a guide of high enough vibration to guard against malevolent entities who may be attracted by the energy raised by the process and by the light which dwells within those who seek to serve others. Each of you, if you are reading these words, carries such a light, and we wish to protect it and you against interference by entities who have malicious interests at mind.

Seek additional resources and education about your guides and the connection process if you are drawn to do so. Should you choose this course, trust your instincts and discernment as to whether those resources and humans who claim the ability to aid you in forging the connection are truly useful and safe for you. Just as not all beings are what they claim, neither are all humans, and even humans with benign intentions may not be what is right for you at that moment.

You know. Within yourselves, you know what is true for you, what you need in your journey, and who can best assist you in attaining your highest ideal. Trust this knowledge above all else, for the path to spiritual growth and to learning to work with those who wish to support you begins with hearing and heeding your own inner wisdom.

    Be well and be loved.

Acknowledgments

This book was so enjoyable to write! And I have a few people—and beings—to thank.

Thank you to Sue, who has been an awesome supporter of my work for a few years now, for the support and the beta reading assistance. Thanks especially for pointing out my tendency toward run-on sentences; I can't promise I managed to eliminate them all, though.

I appreciate the staff at Angels Oasis in Cocoa Village, Florida, for the hints, nudges, reading, and for generally being awesome people. I can't wait to visit your store again! (And to those reading, if you ever find yourself near the Space Coast of Florida, definitely visit Angels Oasis!)

Gratitude to my mentor, whom I won't name here because we have been out of contact for over 14 years now, and he might not appreciate his name showing up here. But without him and his primary guide, I might not have learned that my "invisible friends" are actually my guides, and I almost certainly wouldn't have taken the steps to learn how to channel. He was only part of my life for a very small fraction of time, but he made an immense impact, and I can't let that go unnoted.

Thank you to my awesome partner, Rick, who has been unwaveringly supportive of me (even when I don't make it easy) and of the things I do (even when he doesn't understand them). RiverEvolutions and this book probably wouldn't be a thing if I didn't know him, and I might not even be River Lightbearer.

If I've left out anyone, it wasn't intentional; wibbly-wobbly memory-wemory. I appreciate everyone who has shown me support, listened to me go on about guides and channeling, and given me opportunities to practice my skills.

And thank you, of course, to Shiva, Pietkela, and my other guides for always being there and nudging me to get this book completed!

Bibliography

Andrews, Ted. *How to Meet and Work With Spirit Guides* 2nd edition. Woodbury, Minnesota: Llewellyn Publications 2005

Harris, Christopher S. *Channeling: The Power of Connection.* South Paris, Maine: A New Reality Publishing 2006

Roman, Sanaya, and Duane Packer. *Opening to Channel.* Tiburon, California: H J Kramer Inc. 1987

About the Author

River Lightbearer (they/them) has been on a healing journey most of their adult life and has a passion for helping others heal and find their inner light. As a survivor of abuse and trauma, their heart is in guiding other survivors to gain ground in their journeys and create the lives they want to live. Their compassion, calming energy, and skills with the modality have supported numerous clients in their healing journeys.

Through their practice, River offers channeling and Chios® Energy Healing, both with a "side order" of mindset coaching, online/by distance to clients around the world.

River is a nonbinary eclectic Witch. In addition to this and other books under the River Lightbearer name, they also write or have written under the names Karenna Colcroft, KC Winter, Jo Ramsey, Kimberly Ramsey, and Kim Ramsey-Winkler. They are the mother to two nonbinary offspring and a son-in-law, as well as the grandmother to four wonderful children. River lives in Massachusetts with their husband. When not writing or serving other humans, River is the servant to two cats.

Learn more at https://riverlightbearer.com

RiverEvolutions

RiverEvolutions is the name given to me to use in my practice as catalyst, channel, and healing practitioner, a reflection of my spiritual name, River Lightbearer. Through my work, I help survivors of trauma, as well as others, gain clarity and direction to progress on their healing journeys and throughout their lives.

Channeling is the cornerstone of RiverEvolutions. In a channeling session, you're able to speak, directly or relayed through me, with one of my guides: Shiva, a being of light, or Pietkela, a higher-level being. They share their profound wisdom and compassion to offer guidance and help you identify aspects of your life in which change would benefit you as well as aspects that benefit you now. Pietkela and I also offer guided support to those seeking conscious connection with their own guides.

Chios® Energy Healing, a method of working with your energy to bring positive changes to your mind and body, restores balance and flow to your energy system, bringing you clarity, calmness, and a heightened sense of well-being. I am a Certified Chios® Master Teacher and Chios® Master of Healing Consciousness.

For those who operate their own spiritually-based practices, I offer channeling sessions focused on your business and how best to proceed. As a nonbinary human and a trauma survivor who has done extensive research and studying of the effects of trauma on mind and body, I also offer consultation to practitioners who want to develop a more gender-inclusive and/or trauma-informed practice. And for those seeking an additional service to add to your practice, I provide instruction in the Chios® Energy Healing modality.

Learn more about me and my services by visiting http://www.riverevolutions.com or emailing info@riverevolutions.com.

www.ingramcontent.com/pod-product-compliance
Lightning Source LLC
Chambersburg PA
CBHW060356050426
42449CB00009B/1760